KEYS TO THE KINGDOM

LOCKE&KEY

VOLUME 4

Locke & Key created by Joe Hill and Gabriel Rodriguez

ISBN: 978-1-60010-886-0

14  13  12  11     1  2  3  4

Ted Adams, CEO & Publisher
Greg Goldstein, Chief Operating Officer
Robbie Robbins, EVP/Sr. Graphic Artist
Chris Ryall, Chief Creative Officer/Editor-in-Chief
Matthew Ruzicka, CPA, Chief Financial Officer
Alan Payne, VP of Sales

Become our fan on Facebook **facebook.com/idwpublishing**
Follow us on Twitter **@idwpublishing**
Check us out on YouTube **youtube.com/idwpublishing**
**www.IDWPUBLISHING.com**

Written by: Joe Hill

Art by: Gabriel Rodriguez

Colors by: Jay Fotos

Letters by: Robbie Robbins

Series Edited by: Chris Ryall

Collection Edited by: Justin Eisinger

Collection Designed by: Robbie Robbins

## - KEYS TO THE KINGDOM -

- KEYS TO THE KINGDOM -

Chapter One

# SPARROW

to Bill Watterson

7

10

FIVE MINUTES AGO, WE WERE FRIENDS. NOW HE THINKS I'M LIKE—

A WOLF IN SHEEP'S CLOTHING? FORGET IT. YOU'RE STILL FRIENDS AND HE'LL GET OVER IT. HE WAS GOING TO FIND OUT SOMETIME.

LOOK AT THE SILVER LINING. NO MORE SECRETS. WE CAN BE OUT IN THE OPEN NOW. LIKE IF TYLER WAS STANDING RIGHT HERE WE COULD JUST—

MAYBE YOU'RE RIGHT. MAYBE SECRETS ARE ALWAYS A MISTAKE. LIKE... WHAT WERE YOU AND TY TALKING ABOUT WHEN I WALKED UP? SOUNDED LIKE TY HAS SOME KEY HE ISN'T SHARING.

YOU DON'T WANT TO KNOW ABOUT IT. NOT THIS ONE.

I WISH I HAD TIME TO GO AFTER TYLER. I'D LIKE TO TALK TO HIM, BUT I PROMISED AUNT ELLIE I'D BE HOME EARLY TO HELP WITH RUFUS. IF I DON'T SHOW UP, I'LL BE IN THE DOGHOUSE ALL WEEK.

I'LL HUNT TYLER DOWN. GO ON. TAKE CARE OF WHAT YOU GOT TO TAKE CARE OF.

THANKS. THINK I WILL.

I REALLY *AM* SORRY, TY. I MEAN, I'M *NOT* SORRY THAT I'M WITH ZACK. BUT I AM THAT I DIDN'T FIND A CLASSY WAY TO TELL YOU.

AT LEAST HE'S A GOOD GUY. I HOPE YOU'LL REMEMBER THAT AND NOT DECIDE, JUST 'CAUSE WE'RE GOING OUT, THAT HE'S LIKE A TOTAL MASS MURDERER OR SOMETHING.

WHEREAS I'M NOT SO SURE WE CAN SAY THAT ABOUT YOUR GIRLFRIEND.

22

SHREEE   SHREEE   SHREEE   SHREEE

TY!

KEEP GOING!

SHREEE SHREEE SHREEE SHREEE

SNNNNNGGGG...

UNGH. GET THE FUCK OUTTA MY FACE YOU UGLY—

—BITCH? HEY. HEY.

SHREEE SHREEE SHREEE SHREEE

AAAARRRK!

SHREEE SHREEE SHREEE SHREEE

SHREEE SHREEE SHREEE SHREEE

SHREEE SHREEE SHREEE SHREEE

SHREEE SHREEE SHREEE SHREEE

SHREEE SHREEE SHREEE SHREEE

- KEYS TO THE KINGDOM -

Chapter Two

# WHITE

HOW DOES A FUCKIN' *HALFRICAN* WHO WENT TO A CHURCH SAYIN' 9-11 WAS *VENGEANCE ON THE WHITE MAN*, HOW DOES *THAT* GUY WIND UP TELLIN' ME I GOT TO PAY FOR SOMEONE ELSE'S HEALTH CARE?

I JUST SAID HE COULD PLAY BASKETBALL. I WAS WATCHIN' HIM ON TV. HE GOT A GOOD MOVE TO THE LEFT.

THEY CAN *ALL* PLAY BASKETBALL. WHY I DON'T WATCH THAT SHIT ANYMORE. IT'S DISCRIMINATORY FOR NORMAL WHITE PEOPLE.

I CAN'T HARDLY GET A WHEELCHAIR THROUGH. WERE YOU ALL GOING TO FINISH WITH THIS WALK?

MA'AM, YES, MA'AM. BEAUTIFUL DAY TO SHOVEL FOR MINIMUM WAGE, ISN'T IT, MIZ BLAXTON?

*BRIXTON*, MR. PARSONS. IF YOU HAVE TROUBLE READING MY NAME TAG, YOU SHOULD POKE YOUR HEAD IN THE CONTINUING EDUCATION OFFICE. THEY OFFER DISCOUNTS FOR STAFF ON PRIVATE MENTORING.

CONGRATS ON ANOTHER WIN. TOO BAD FENCING IS SUCH A WEENIE SPORT. IT'S EVEN MORE DINKY THAN LACROSSE AND ROUGHLY AS COOL AS BEING IN THE *WORLD OF WARCRAFT* CLUB.

*I* THINK IT'S COOL.

HER APPROVAL ACTUALLY SUPPORTS MY ARGUMENT.

33

McCLELLAN PSYCHIATRIC HOSPITAL

TYLER. THAT WOMAN. SHE MIGHT KNOW SOMETHING ABOUT DAD. AND KEYHOUSE. AND... AND...

AND NOTHING. LET IT GO.

LET IT GO? WHAT ARE YOU THINKING?

I'M THINKING SHIT IS ALMOST NORMAL FOR ONCE AND I KIND OF LIKE IT. I'M THINKING I'VE ALREADY HAD ENOUGH CRAZY IN MY LIFE.

WATCH ME.

YOU PLAY NANCY DREW IF YOU HAVE TO. JUST DEAL ME OUT.

TYLER. WE CAN'T WALK AWAY FROM THIS.

I NEED TO GET IN THERE. I NEED TO TALK TO HER.

WHY? I MEAN, YES, SHE KNEW YOUR FATHER, THAT SEEMS EVIDENT. BUT—

SHE DIDN'T JUST KNOW HIM. THEY WERE FRIENDS. BEST FRIENDS.

YOU CAN'T KNOW THAT. DID YOUR DAD EVER SAY ANYTHING ABOUT ERIN VOSS TO YOU?

DIDN'T NEED TO.

"SHE WAS ON THE WALL. DOWN IN THE DROWNING CAVE."

BY THE TIME WE GOT OUT OF THE CAVE, I HAD MOSTLY FORGOTTEN ABOUT WHAT WAS ON THE WALL. GOT A LITTLE DISTRACTED TRYING NOT TO DROWN.

BUT WHEN HER NURSE SAID HER NAME, IT ALL CAME BACK TO ME.

I GUESS I STILL DON'T GET WHY YOU WANT TO TALK TO HER. I MEAN, EVEN IF SHE **WAS** CLOSE TO YOUR FATHER IN HIGH SCHOOL... WHAT COULD SHE POSSIBLY TELL YOU THAT YOU NEED TO KNOW ABOUT?

MY DAD DIDN'T TALK MUCH ABOUT GOING TO LOVECRAFT ACADEMY. I ALWAYS THOUGHT IT WAS BECAUSE HIS MOTHER DIED WHEN HE WAS IN HIGH SCHOOL AND HE WAS SAD ABOUT IT.

BUT THERE WAS SOMETHING ELSE. I **KNOW** THERE WAS SOMETHING ELSE. AND I THINK THIS ERIN VOSS MIGHT BE ABLE TO TELL ME WHAT.

EVEN IF SHE DOES KNOW SOMETHING, AND YOU COULD GET IN THERE, DOESN'T SOUND LIKE SHE'D WANT TO SHARE IT WITH YOU...

...*WHITEY*.

THAT WAS THE WORST PART. SHE COULDN'T HANDLE THE SIGHT OF US. SHE LOOKED AT US AND SAW A LYNCH MOB.

IN HER MIND WE WERE... *CRIMINALS*— WE WERE *DANGEROUS*— JUST 'CAUSE OF THE COLOR OF OUR SKIN. HOW SCREWED UP IS THAT?

THERE ARE SO MANY IRONIC STATEMENTS I COULD INSERT INTO THE CONVERSATION AT THIS POINT, I CAN'T CHOOSE BETWEEN THEM.

NOW WAIT A MINUTE THERE, MATE. YOU'RE TALKING ABOUT RACISM. THE PROBLEM WITH THE DAME IN McCLELLAN IS THAT SHE'S COMPLETELY MENTAL.

I RATHER THINK ONE THING IS DIFFERENT FROM THE OTHER.

SURE, IT'S DIFFERENT. 'CAUSE THE SHOE IS ON THE OTHER FOOT.

WHITE PEOPLE AREN'T USED TO DUDES MAKING BROAD, SWEEPING GENERALIZATIONS ABOUT THEM. THEY'RE MORE COMFORTABLE BEING THE ONES WHO GENERALIZE. THE MAJORITY ALWAYS IS.

I KIND OF WALKED INTO THIS ONE, HUH?

STILL. IT'S FUNNY TO THINK ERIN VOSS USED TO BE FRIENDS WITH MY DAD— WHO WAS SO WHITE HE'D SING ALONG TO PETER CETERA—AND NOW THE SIGHT OF WHITE PEOPLE IS ENOUGH TO KICK OFF A SCREAMING FIT.

I HAVE TO GET IN THERE. EITHER OF YOU HAVE ANY IDEA WHERE I CAN GET A GRAPPLING HOOK AND SOME ROPE?

YOU CAN SKIP THAT. IT'S NOT EXACTLY A HIGH-SECURITY INSTALLATION. MY UNCLE USED TO WORK THERE.

NO SHIT? LIKE AS WHAT? JANITOR OR SOMETHING?

YOU'RE SO *SIMPLE*. YOU JUST LIKE TO STICK YOUR DICK IN THINGS AND GENTLY STIR.

MY UNCLE WAS A PAYROLL ACCOUNTANT—*SHITHEAD*—BACK WHEN IT WAS STILL A GOOD GIG.

BUT IT'S A LOUSY NEIGHBORHOOD. THAT WHOLE AREA IS OLD AND WHITE AND IRISH AND BROKE AND ANGRY. PEOPLE DRIVING AROUND WITH BUMPER STICKERS THAT SAY "SOMEWHERE IN AFRICA, A VILLAGE IS MISSING ITS IDIOT."

SECOND TIME SOMEONE SCRATCHED "NIGGER" ON THE HOOD OF MY UNCLE'S OLDS, HE SAID "GOOD ENOUGH" AND CALLED IT QUITS.

PEOPLE SUCK.

WHEN HE STILL WORKED THERE, THOUGH, HE USED TO HAVE ME OVER SATURDAY NIGHTS TO VOLUNTEER. KIDS COME BY TO READ BOOKS TO THE OLDER FOLKS. IF YOU'VE GOT A COPY OF *BELOVED* IN YOUR HAND, YOU CAN WALTZ RIGHT IN.

ALL RIGHT. SATURDAY, THEN.

BUT KINSEY, LUV— EVEN IF YOU GET IN, SO WHAT? YOU ALREADY KNOW SHE ISN'T GOING TO TALK TO YOU. LOOK IN THE MIRROR...

...YOU'RE STILL WHITE.

THE FUCK YOU TALKING ABOUT? LEATHERFACE WOULD KICK THE *SHIT* OUT OF FREDDY KRUEGER. IT'S UNREALISTIC TO EVEN *IMAGINE* IT'D BE A FIGHT.

THE *CHAINSAW* GUY HAS 150 POUNDS ON ROBERT ENGLUND, EASY. NOW I'M A BIG MOTHERFUCKER. I DON'T CARE IF A GUY *DOES* HAVE KNIVES FOR FINGERS. NOT GOOD ENOUGH.

YOU PUT ME IN A RING WITH SOME WHIPPY-THIN BITCH LIKE FREDDY, I DON'T CARE IF HE'S GOT A *FISTFUL* OF KNIVES. LET HIM POKE ME A COUPLE TIMES. I'LL TAKE HIS LITTLE STICKERS AWAY AND KNIFE-FUCK HIM IN THE ASS.

HAVE YOU EVER EVEN *SEEN* ANY OF THESE MOVIES? LIKE, FREDDY—HE'S MADE OUT OF *BAD DREAMS*. HE'D COME OUT OF NOWHERE AND YANK YOU INTO HIS NIGHTMARE WORLD WHEN YOU LEAST EXPECT IT.

WHAT ARE YOU TALKIN ABOUT, *YANK* ME INTO THE NIGHTMARE WORLD?

I ALREADY MOP THE FLOORS THERE. MY WHOLE SHITTY LIFE IS ONE BIG, LONG, UNDERPAID BAD DREAM, PULLIN' WEEKEND SHIFTS IN MCCLELLAN, SURROUNDED BY PANTS-SHITTING LUNATICS AND TAKIN' ORDERS FROM SMART-MOUTH, OVEREDUCATED NIG—

MCCLELLAN. YOU WORK THERE, DON'T YOU?

HEL—LO THERE.

UNNNH... WHAT'D YOU SAY?

MCCLELLAN HOSPITAL. I NOTICED YOUR OUTFITS WHEN I CAME IN.

WHAT?

IF I FIX IT SO YOU CAN TALK TO HER, YOU HAVE TO GIVE ME BACK THE HEAD KEY AND YOU HAVE TO TAKE ME WITH YOU AND YOU HAVE TO INCLUDE ME WHEN YOU MAKE PLANS, FROM NOW ON, FOREVER.

WHAT ARE YOU TALKING ABOUT? WHEN WE MAKE PLANS? WHAT DO YOU HAVE BEHIND YOUR BACK?

YOU AND TYLER. WHEN YOU TALK ABOUT THE HOUSE AND THE CAVE AND THE OMEGA KEY AND THE BAD LADY, YOU DON'T EVER INCLUDE ME BECAUSE YOU THINK I'M SCARED BUT I'M NOT SCARED I WANT TO BE PART OF IT AND THAT'S THE DEAL.

HOW ARE YOU GOING TO FIX IT SO I CAN TALK TO ERIN VOSS?

WHAT IS THAT? WHERE'D YOU FIND IT?

AROUND. REMEMBER I GAVE YOUR HAND-MIRROR AWAY TO THE GIRL IN THE WELL? YOU CAN HAVE THIS ONE. IT'LL MAKE IT SO ERIN VOSS WILL WANT TO TALK TO YOU.

CLAC!

IF I CAN GET CLOSE ENOUGH TO HER, I DON'T *NEED* TO TALK TO HER. I CAN JUST USE THE HEAD KEY TO— WAIT A MINUTE. HOW IS THAT GOING TO HELP ME?

OH. EM.

GEE.

WHAT A WASTE OF RESOURCES YOU ARE, WOMAN. DO YOU DO ANYTHING BESIDES SLEEP AND EAT?

ACTUALLY—HEH. THAT'S LIKE 90% OF THE BLACK PEOPLE I KNOW, RIGHT THERE.

ALL RIGHT. TIME TO SMILE AND SAY "BOOBIES," YOU OUL' BITCH.

HELLO, ERIN.

MMMNNNN!

I WOULD'VE COME SOONER, BUT YOU KNOW HOW THE ANYWHERE KEY WORKS. I HAVE TO BE ABLE TO VISUALIZE WHERE I'M GOING.

OR DO YOU KNOW? THAT'S THE PROBLEM, ISN'T IT? I THOUGHT I CLEANED YOU OUT. YOU SHOULDN'T KNOW ANYTHING. BUT YOU SAW TYLER AND THOUGHT "RENDELL."

IF YOU REMEMBER ANYTHING, IT'S A PROBLEM. I CAN'T HAVE ANY RISKS TO MY IDENTITY. NOT WHEN I'M SO CLOSE TO OPENING THE BLACK DOOR AND BRINGING THEM THROUGH.

NO. NO. P-PLEASE. IT'S—IT'S— WHITE.

45

MISS VOSS?

WHITE. IT'S *WHITE*. DODGE.

MISS VOSS, THIS IS A TERRIBLE INVASION OF YOUR PRIVACY... IT'S JUST THE ONLY *WAY*. IF MY WHOLE FAMILY WASN'T IN DANGER, I WOULDN'T, I WOULDN'T *EVER*. BUT... IF YOU REALLY WERE MY DAD'S FRIEND, I KNOW YOU'D WANT TO HELP US.

DODGE. *DODGE*.

THANK YOU.

AFTER YOU CHANGED BACK, DID—

YEAH. GOT A CAB, NO PROBLEM.

...ARMED PROTESTORS MARCHED OUTSIDE A CIVIL RIGHTS MEMORIAL ATTENDED BY THE PRESIDENT...

AS NORTH KOREA AND JA

...NEW STUDY SUGGESTS AFRICAN-AMERICANS WAIT UP TO FOURTEEN MINUTES LONGER IN THE EMERGENCY ROOM BEFORE RECEIVING TREATMENT...

AT LEAST THEY DON'T KNOW WHAT YOU LOOK LIKE. YOU DON'T HAVE TO WORRY ABOUT THE POLICE TYING YOU INTO A PAIR OF MURDERS. THEY'RE LOOKING FOR TWO BLACK KIDS. SO THAT'S GOOD.

DISCUSSION CONTINUES, NEW HEALTH PLANS

THAT'S A *GOOD* THING? REALLY? TWO MEN GET KILLED AND WHO ARE THE COPS GOING TO BLAME FOR IT? A COUPLE BLACK KIDS. SAME AS ALWAYS. RIGHT?

WELL... *NO*... I MEAN... THAT PART OF IT *SUCKS*, BUT I'M JUST SAYING...

...ARE YOU OKAY?

STILL HA
O KEEP THEIR JOBS

...THE ECONOMIC RECOVERY HAS NOT YET REACHED THE INNER CITY...

I DON'T KNOW HOW TO FEEL SAD ANYMORE. THIS IS THE FIRST TIME I'VE EVER THOUGHT IT MIGHT NOT BE A GOOD THING.

SO THE GUY IN ERIN VOSS'S HEAD...

MCCLELLAN PSYCHIATRIC HOSPITAL

INVESTIGATION IS FOLLOWING SEVERAL LEADS

SHE NEVER SAW HIS FACE, SO I COULDN'T. THERE WAS NOTHING UNDER HIS SKI MASK. ALL I KNOW IS SHE CALLED HIM DODGE AND SHE WAS SCARED OF HIM.

BUT—

WAIT. *SH.* HERE IT IS.

...AFTERMATH OF THIS HORRIFIC SLAYING, POLICE ARE LOOKING FOR AN AFRICAN-AMERICAN, IN HER TEENS OR EARLY TWENTIES...

3NEWS

...IF YOU'VE SEEN SOMEONE WHO MATCHES THIS DESCRIPTION, CALL THE POLICE AND DO NOT ATTEMPT TO APPROACH YOURSELF, AS SHE SHOULD BE CONSIDERED ARMED AND VERY, *VERY* DANGEROUS...

SSION ABOUT MURDER RATES IN THE EAST COAST THIS WINTER KEE

- KEYS TO THE KINGDOM -

Chapter Three

# FEBRUARY

FEBRUARY
**02**
THU

I JUST WISH SHE DIDN'T START CRYING WHEN SHE SAW ME. THAT'S THE PART I REALLY HATE.

YOUR MOTHER STARTED CRYING WHEN SHE SAW YOU? WHAT THE FUCK IS THAT?

SHE OVERREACTS TO EVERYTHING THESE DAYS.

IF IT CHEERS YOU UP, I THINK A COUPLE BRUISES MAKE A GUY LOOK DANGEROUS. IN A CUTE SORT OF WAY.

BESIDES. I SEE A BLACK EYE AND I JUST WANT TO KISS IT BETTER.

PAY ATTENTION TO WHAT JORDAN IS SAYING, DUDE. SHE LIKES MEN WHO ARE DAMAGED. THEY'RE EASIER PREY.

EAT MY ASS, BRINKER.

KEEP YOUR FANTASIES TO YOURSELF, BABE.

I WAS THINKING ABOUT A GOLD TOOTH FOR THE ONE I LOST. I DUNNO? STUPID OR BADASS?

BADASS. FOR SURE. YOU NEED A GOLD TOOTH AND YOU NEED TO GET RID OF THIS NASTY CAP WITH THAT FUCKING HILLBILLY HOOK—

MY CAP AND LURE? OH, NO, SORRY. I CAN'T. SEE, THE LURE WAS REALLY SPECIAL TO MY DAD AND I PROMISED I'D HOLD ONTO IT FOR A DAY WHEN I NEEDED SOME LUCK. AND THE HAT IS FROM THE DAY GIAMBI WENT 5 FOR 5 AND...

THIS IS RED SOX COUNTRY, DUDE, AND I HATE THAT FUCKING HAT AND THAT STUPID HOOK. TELL YOU WHAT. YOU THROW THEM AWAY, RIGHT NOW, *BOTH* OF THEM, AND WHEN WE GO TO THE BEACH TOMORROW NIGHT, I'LL—

56

FEBRUARY
**04**
SAT

I *DO*, I LOVE TYLER. BUT I AGREE WITH YOU. IT WOULD BE SAFER IF SOMEONE ELSE KNEW WHAT HE DID WITH THIS—WHAT'D YOU CALL IT? OMEGA KEY? NOW IF SOMEONE *ELSE* KNOWS WHERE IT'S HIDDEN, THEN NO MATTER WHAT...

OH, CAN WE *STOP* TALKING ABOUT TYLER AND THE OMEGA KEY AND THE DARK LADY? I DIDN'T HAVE YOU OVER FOR A BUNCH OF TALK. I WANT TO DO SOMETHING *FUN*.

LIKE... FUN HOW? WHAT KIND OF FUN? I LIKE FUN.

ME TOO. AND IT'S TIME.

I WANT YOU TO OPEN UP TO ME. I WANT TO TAKE ONE OF YOUR HAPPIEST THOUGHTS AND PUT IT IN MY HEAD, AND I'LL TAKE ONE OF *MY* HAPPIEST THOUGHTS AND—

*NO.* THERE'S NO WAY.

WHY NOT? YOU CAN TRUST ME. YOU'VE SEEN ALL THE BAD STUFF IN *MY* HEAD. THERE CAN'T BE ANYTHING HALF SO BAD IN YOURS.

PLEASE. IT'LL FEEL GOOD. WHY CAN'T WE MAKE EACH OTHER FEEL GOOD?

FORGET IT. MY HEAD IS OFF-LIMITS.

YEAH. YOU'RE HAPPY TO GET YOUR HANDS UNDER MY SHIRT, BUT I'M NOT ALLOWED TO TOUCH *YOUR* OFF-LIMIT BITS.

I'VE NOTICED YOU DON'T WANT ME TO GET TOO CLOSE. TELL YOU WHAT, LET ME MAKE IT EASY FOR YOU TO PROTECT YOUR PRIVACY. GET OUT.

DAMMIT, I WISH I COULD STILL CRY.

59

FEBRUARY
05
SUN

FINE! I'M FINE! I CAN'T EVEN FEEL 'EM. IT'S NO BIG DEAL. I JUST TRIPPED!

INTO WHAT? A BAG OF CATS?

FEBRUARY
**06**
MON

MISHAP? MISHAP WITH WHAT? A CRATE FULL OF SCISSORS?

WILL YOU RELAX? YOU'RE CHANNELING MY MOTHER.

FEBRUARY
**07**
TUE

FEBRUARY
**08**
WED

OUT WITH IT, LUV. NO MORE PREVARICATIONS. WHAT HAPPENED TO YOU? YOU LOOK LIKE YOU LOST A CAGE MATCH WITH A PILE OF FORKS.

IT'S... *COMPLICATED.* AND... *WEIRD.* AND AFTER WHAT HAPPENED DOWN IN THE CAVE, I'M NOT GOING TO PULL YOU TWO INTO ANY MORE TROUBLE.

WHOA. YOU NEED TO STOP RIGHT THERE. YOU DON'T NEED TO PROTECT US FROM SHIT. FROM THE LOOKS OF YOU, *YOU'RE* THE ONE NEEDS PROTECTING.

IT'S NOT JUST ABOUT PROTECTING YOU. ALTHOUGH THERE IS THAT. BUT I ALSO DON'T WANT TO FRIGHTEN YOU GUYS OFF.

I JUST HAD THIS BIG, STUPID BREAK-UP WITH ZACK. I CAN'T LOSE ANYMORE FRIENDS RIGHT NOW.

YOU AND ZACK BROKE UP? OH, THAT'S... SO DREADFULLY...

...WONDERFUL.

DID YOU BREAK-UP BECAUSE HE COULDN'T HANDLE "WEIRD" AND "COMPLICATED"?

KIND OF. I PILED A LOT OF STRANGE SHIT ON HIM, AND HE WAS VERY COOL AND VERY ACCEPTING ABOUT IT.

BUT THEN I ASKED HIM TO TRUST ME ON SOMETHING AND IT WAS SCARY AND HE COULDN'T AND I WAS WRONG TO ASK.

SAME AS IT WOULD BE WRONG TO ASK YOU GUYS.

'EY, MATE, DID YOU JUST MAKE LITTLE QUOTATION SIGNS WITH YOUR FINGERS? THAT IS SO CUTE.

I GUESS I SHOULD TELL ZACK I'M SORRY, HUH?

NOT AT ALL. HE SHOULD APOLOGIZE TO YOU, FOR BEING AN INCORRIGIBLE PUSSY. FUCK HIM. WHATEVER HE WOULDN'T TRUST YOU ON—WHATEVER HE WAS AFRAID TO DO—I'D DO IT. TWICE.

A-FUCKING-MEN.

I... PROMISED JACKIE AFTER THE CAVE THAT I WOULDN'T PUT ANY OF YOU GUYS AT RISK AGAIN.

YEAH, WELL, I DIDN'T PROMISE ANYTHING.

ME, NEITHER. I HARDLY TAKE MY MARCHING ORDERS FROM MISS JACKIE VEDA AND I'M NOT AFRAID TO SAY SO TO HER—

HELLO, DEARS, WHAT'S UP THIS FINE DAY?

NOTHING!

LOVE ALL THE CLOSET SPACE IN THIS HOUSE.

WHAT'CHU LOOKING AT BODE?

NOTHING... MUCH.

FEBRUARY
09
THU

OH, HELL. WHAT IS IT THIS TIME?

WHEN MOM OPENED IT THERE WAS NOTHING IN THERE. BUT SHE JUST USED ONE OF THE HOUSE KEYS FROM THE HARDWARE STORE.

BUT YOU USE THIS...

CLiC

...IT'S LIKE OPENING THE DOOR TO THE BATCAVE.

FEBRUARY
**10**
FRI

FEBRUARY
**11**
SAT

KINSEY! IT'S SCOT! WE'VE GOT TO PUT IT *BACK*!

WE'VE GOT TO CAPTURE SCOT AND PUT HIS *SANITY* BACK BEFORE HE GETS HIMSELF EXPELLED! HE'S PERFORMING BYRON ON THE QUAD!

YEAH? SO?

•FEBRUARY
**13**
MON

I CAN'T BELIEVE YOU'D JUST DRAG THEM INTO THIS WITHOUT TALKING TO ME! SOMETIMES I THINK YOU USED THE HEAD KEY TO TAKE OUT YOUR LAST FEW REMAINING I.Q. POINTS!

LOVE GETTING THIS LECTURE FROM A GUY WHO COULDN'T WAIT TO WHIP OUT HIS BIG MAGIC KEY TO IMPRESS SOME GIRL HE BARELY KNEW.

•FEBRUARY
**14**
TUE

HAPPY VALENTINE'S DAY, TY. MAKE IT SPECIAL, WHY DON'T YOU? TAKE YOUR LEFT HAND FOR A ROMANTIC NIGHT OUT.

66

KINSEY, GIRL. I'VE DECIDED I HAVE ANOTHER MEMORY I WANT TO SHARE WITH—

JAMAL? SAY WHAT... WHAT ARE YOU TWO...

OH, HEY, DUDE. I WAS JUST—WE BEEN TRADING MEMORIES OF OUR DADS ALL AFTERNOON. IT'S AWESOME. SO AWESOME.

KINSEY? YOU AND HIM ARE—I THOUGHT THAT WAS... WAS OUR THING.

SCOT, WE'RE JUST FOOLING AROUND A LITTLE. IT'S NOT—IT'S NO BIG DEAL.

AND I THOUGHT WE WERE MATES, MATE.

NO, YOU THOUGHT I WAS YOUR FUNNY ETHNIC SIDEKICK. OR YOUR CHEERLEADER. OR SOMETHING. FAR AS I'M CONCERNED, YOU DISQUALIFIED YOUR CLAIM TO KINSEY WHEN YOU WERE WILLING TO LET HER DROWN TO SAVE YOUR OWN ASS, AND ME WITH HER.

GUYS... JAMAL, THAT'S NOT FAIR... SCOT... NEITHER OF YOU HAVE A CLAIM...

FEBRUARY 23 THU

HOW THEY BITING?

GOOD. JUST PULLED IN A MACKEREL. SIX POUNDS, AT LEAST.

MUST BE NICE. NOT BEING ABLE TO CRY. I GOT TO GIVE THAT A WHIRL.

NO, YOU DON'T. I WISH I HADN'T DONE IT. MAYBE IF I COULD STILL REMEMBER WHAT IT'S LIKE TO FEEL SAD, I WOULDN'T HAVE GONE AND FUCKED THINGS UP WITH MY BEST FRIENDS.

JAMAL AND SCOT WON'T TALK TO EACH OTHER ANY MORE AND JACKIE TOLD ME SHE CAN'T BE FRIENDS WITH SOMEONE SO... RECKLESS WITH OTHER PEOPLE'S TRUST. AND SHE'S RIGHT. WHAT A MESS I MADE, TYLER.

HEY. I THOUGHT YOU WERE OPPOSED TO USING THE KEYS EXCEPT WHEN WE'RE UNDER ATTACK. WHY ARE YOU WEARING THAT?

BECAUSE I'M SICK OF FEELING WEAK.

OH, TY. I DON'T KNOW. THAT THING MAKES YOU—WHAT—THREE TIMES AS STRONG AS YOU USUALLY ARE?

IT'S NOT THE KIND OF THING YOU JUST WANT TO WALK AROUND IN. SOMEONE COULD GET HURT.

YEAH. THAT'S PRETTY MUCH WHAT I WAS THINKING.

- KEYS TO THE KINGDOM -

Chapter Four

# CASUALTIES

THAT'S A REALLY CUTE BRITISH ACCENT, BODE. YOU BEEN PRACTICING?

UH-HUH. WITH SCOT. AND ZACK IS GOING TO TEACH ME FENCING SO I CAN SWORDFIGHT WITH A BRITISH ACCENT.

HEY, KINSEY, HOW COME THEY HAVEN'T BEEN OVER LATELY? LIKE SCOT OR ZACK OR JAMAL... OR... OR JACKIE... OR ANYONE?

BECAUSE I WASN'T A VERY GOOD FRIEND, BODE.

KINSEY? ARE YOU OKAY?

YOU KNOW ME, KID. NOTHING MUCH GETS ME DOWN ANYMORE. YOU THINK YOU CAN HELP ME WITH SOMETHING?

I PROMISED COACH WHEDON I'D WATCH RUFUS THIS AFTERNOON. SHE'S BUSY WITH ASSESSMENTS. ZACK CAN'T WATCH HIM BECAUSE IT'S SUNDAY AND HE GOES TO BOSTON ON THE WEEKEND FOR HIS RESEARCH PAPER.

JACKIE WATCHES HIM SOMETIMES, BUT SHE'S OFF LOOKING AT YALE THIS WEEKEND. SO IT'S JUST ME. CAN YOU GO ON MISSIONS WITH RUFUS? I THINK HE'D LIKE THAT.

QUITE, QUITE.

I'LL BE BACK WITH COCOA. YOU TWO MAKE FRIENDS.

THAT OUGHT TO BE EASY. ALL WE NEED IS A BUNCHA BANANAS FOR MONKEYFACE HERE.

I'VE HAD TO WORK WITH SOME SORRY RECRUITS BEFORE BUT GETTING A GORILLA ASSIGNED TO SQUADRON STRANGE IS THE LAST STRAW!

NOW, NOW, OLD CHAP. I DON'T MUCH LIKE GOING TO WAR BESIDE AN ARMED VACUUM CLEANER, BUT WE DON'T GET TO PICK WHO WE FIGHT WITH... OR THE THINGS WE FIGHT AGAINST.

THE COSTUMED APE MAKES A LOGICAL POINT. WE SHOULD FIND A SECURE POSITION AND PREPARE TO DEFEND OURSELVES.

GOOD IDEA. LET'S REGROUP AT HEADQUARTERS.

SOUNDS LIKE A PLAN.

AS LONG AS HEADQUARTERS ISN'T DARK. I'M A LITTLE SCARED OF THE DARK.

OH, HELLO. WERE WE BEING TOO LOUD?

YOU AREN'T BOTHERING ME.

YOU CAN SEE ME?

YES, SIR.

KNOCK KNOCK!

WHO'S THERE?

MY OLD PAL SMITH AND HIS BUDDY, MR. WESTON! *BLAM! BLAMABLAM BLAMBLAM!*

YOU HEAR MY VOICE?

I'M READING YOU LOUD AND CLEAR, SIR.

THIS IS A SECURE ZONE. YOU'LL HAVE TO IDENTIFY YOURSELF. NAME, RANK, AND SERIAL NUMBER.

NAME, RANK, AND... SERGEANT SAMUEL LESSER, U.S. ARMY. SERIAL NUMBER... 867-5309. CURRENTLY DECEASED. DO YOU KNOW WHAT DECEASED MEANS?

SIR, YES SIR.

IF YOU DON'T MIND CHEWING THE FAT WITH A LOWLY PRIVATE, I'LL FALL IN WITH YOU.

NOT HERE, THOUGH. OTHER PEOPLE CAN'T SEE ME. THEY MIGHT WONDER WHO YOU'RE TALKING TO.

I DON'T KNOW IF ANYONE WILL CARE, SIR. EVERYONE ALREADY THINKS I'M SECTION-8.

BESIDES, I PROMISED KINSEY I'D STAY IN THE PARLOR. SHE'S THE REGIONAL COMMANDER HERE.

YOU CAN DISREGARD HER ORDERS, PRIVATE. I OUTRANK HER.

YOU SEE MY STRIPES DON'T YOU?

SIR, YES SIR. JUST... WE'RE HAVING COCOA AND BLUEBERRY COBBLER AT 1900 HOURS.

I'LL GET YOU BACK BY THEN.

WELL... ALL RIGHT.

MY WORD, I BELIEVE THESE BRONTOSAURI CAN BE TRAINED!

AFTER YOU'RE DONE, I WANT YOU TO TAKE THE KEY TO THE WINE CELLAR. JUST PUT IT SOMEPLACE I WON'T FIND IT. CAN YOU DO THAT?

SHOULDN'T BE A PROBLEM.

YOUR NAME IS RUFUS. YOU'RE THE TRACK COACH'S SON. YOU LIVE WITH THE ONE CALLED ZACK WELLS.

THAT'S AFFIRMATIVE, SIR. WHAT ABOUT YOUR FAMILY? DO THEY KNOW WHAT HAPPENED TO YOU?

DO YOU KNOW WHO KILLED THEM?

WHAT ABOUT YOU, RUFUS? DID YOU CUT SOME KIND OF DEAL WITH HIM?

WITH WHO?

I DON'T KNOW WHO YOU'RE TALKING ABOUT. I DON'T KNOW ANY REAL ENEMIES.

YES. I'M AFRAID I DO. SOMEONE WHO THOUGHT HE COULD CUT A DEAL WITH THE ENEMY. BUT THERE ARE NO DEALS WITH HIM.

THE PERSON WHO KILLED THEM IS GONE NOW.

SOMETIMES I FIGHT VELOCIRAPTOR MEN AND SOMETIMES I FIGHT SADDAM HUSSEIN, BUT THEY'RE JUST PRETEND.

THE ENEMY I'M TALKING ABOUT LIVES IN THE SAME HOUSE WITH YOU. HE'S NOT WHAT HE APPEARS TO BE. HE LOOKS LIKE A BOY, BUT HE'S NOT.

HE'S BOTH MORE THAN THAT, AND QUITE A BIT LESS. AND...

...HE'S WATCHING YOU RIGHT NOW!

DON'T BE AFRAID. HE SEES YOU, BUT HE CAN'T SEE ME, AND HE CAN'T HEAR EITHER OF US. HE DOESN'T KNOW WE'RE TALKING.

IF HE THINKS ANYTHING, HE THINKS YOU'RE TALKING TO YOUR TOYS.

WHY IS HE WATCHING ME? HOW CAN HE DO THAT?

DON'T BE AFRAID. HE'S SEARCHING FOR SOMETHING. HE'S BEEN LOOKING OVER THE HOUSE ALL NIGHT, AND AT THE MOMENT HE'S LOOKING AT YOU.

HE MAY ALSO BE KEEPING AN EYE ON YOU BECAUSE HE KNOWS YOU'RE DANGEROUS TO HIM.

I TOLD YOU THIS HOUSE IS A BATTLEGROUND BUT I DIDN'T SAY WHAT'S BEING FOUGHT FOR HERE. MAYBE I SHOULD SHOW YOU.

FALL IN, SOLDIER.

OOO, I... I DON'T LIKE THE DARK. REQUEST PERMISSION TO ABORT MISSION.

NEGATIVE, SOLDIER...

...I BROUGHT A LIGHT.

WHAT IS THIS PLACE?

THE CHAMBER OF THE LIVING SHADOWS.

IS IT... IS IT SAFE?

THE SHADOWS SERVE WHOEVER HOLDS THE SHADOW KEY AND WEARS THE SHADOW CROWN. SOMETIMES RELUCTANTLY, BUT ALWAYS FAITHFULLY.

ZACK WELLS IS USING A DIFFERENT KEY TO OBSERVE YOU, EVEN AT THIS MOMENT. THIS HOUSE IS FULL OF IMPOSSIBLE KEYS.

THEY ARE BOTH THE WEAPONS IN THE WAR, AND THE VALUABLES BEING FOUGHT OVER.

I'M SCARED. I DON'T LIKE IT HERE. I THINK I SHOULD GO. I THINK I WANT TO GO HOME.

HOME IS BETTER? WITH HIM LIVING THERE?

YOUR MOTHER MUST KNOW THE TRUTH ABOUT HIM. SHE MUST KNOW HOW DANGEROUS HE IS. AND YET SHE SHELTERS HIM. GIVES AID AND COMFORT...*TO THE ENEMY.*

HE'LL USE HER UNTIL SHE CAN'T SERVE HIM ANYMORE, THEN CUT HER DOWN. THAT'S WHAT HE DOES WITH HIS SERVANTS.

STOP CRYING, RUFUS. IT'S TIME TO BE A MAN.

I JUST WANT HIM TO GO AWAY, BUT I DON'T KNOW WHAT TO DO. THERE'S NOTHING I CAN DO.

YES, THERE IS, RUFUS. THIS IS WAR.

KILL HIM.

SLIP A KNIFE IN HIS RIBS WHILE HE'S ASLEEP. GIVE YOUR MOTHER—GIVE US ALL—A HAPPY ENDING.

SIR, NO SIR. NOT WHILE HE'S ASLEEP. THAT WOULD VIOLATE THE TERMS OF THE GENEVA CONVENTION.

ALSO, I'M NOT ALLOWED TO TOUCH THE KNIVES IN THE KITCHEN. IT'S ON THE CHALKBOARD WITH ALL MY RULES.

WHAT IS THIS STUFF, SIR?

AN INSTRUMENT PANEL THAT OPERATES A VERY OLD PUMP. IT CONTROLS THE WATER LEVEL IN THE CAVES BELOW THE HOUSE. I SAID I'D TELL YOU WHAT THIS IS ALL ABOUT. WHAT HE'S LOOKING FOR.

THE ENEMY WANTS SOMETHING THAT'S DOWN IN THOSE CAVES, RUFUS. RIGHT NOW, THEY'RE FLOODED. BUT HE CAN USE THE VALVES TO DRAIN THEM.

THERE'S A KEY—THE MOST DANGEROUS KEY OF ALL—THAT UNLOCKS A DOOR IN THAT CAVE. HE WANTS TO OPEN IT. HE WANTS WHAT'S ON THE OTHER SIDE.

WHAT'S ON THE OTHER SIDE, SIR?

REINFORCEMENTS.

ZACK WELLS IS CONTROLLED BY A PARASITE OF THE SPIRIT... WHAT THEY WOULD'VE CALLED A DEMON IN A LESS SCIENTIFIC AGE. IF HE COULD BRING THROUGH EVEN ONE MORE, THEY COULD MULTIPLY.

HE COULD MAKE EVERYONE IN THE WORLD LIKE HIM.

HE'S BEEN SEARCHING FOR THE KEY FOR MONTHS. SOONER OR LATER, HE'LL GET IT, UNLESS SOMEONE FINDS A WAY TO TAKE HIM OUT OF THE PICTURE.

I CAN'T KILL HIM, NO SIR. KILLING IS BAD. EVERYONE KNOWS THAT. EXCEPT IN MAKE-BELIEVE.

I DIDN'T KNOW YOU WERE A CONSCIENTIOUS OBJECTOR, SOLDIER. BUT... THERE ARE OTHER WAYS TO DEAL WITH HIM.

WHAT WAYS?

SIR? IT'S COLD, SIR.

IS IT?

I'M NOT DRESSED FOR ALL—WEATHER MANEUVERS.

WE WON'T BE OUT HERE LONG. KINSEY AND BODE ARE ALREADY LOOKING FOR YOU. THEY'RE WORRIED ABOUT YOU.

THINGS HAVE A WAY OF DISAPPEARING IN THIS HOUSE.

KEYS. CHILDREN.

I DON'T WANT TO SCARE ANYONE. I SHOULD GO BACK.

WOULDN'T IT BE SOMETHING IF WE COULD USE THIS PLACE TO MAKE *ZACK WELLS* DISAPPEAR?

YES, SIR. YOU SAID THERE WAS SOME WAY TO DEAL WITH HIM THAT WOULDN'T BE THE SAME AS KILLING HIM. WHAT WOULD THAT BE, SIR?

I'M LEANING AGAINST IT.

ZACK WELLS DOESN'T BELONG IN OUR WORLD. HE'S AN ECHO OF SOMEONE WHO LIVED AND DIED A LONG TIME AGO. SOMEONE INFECTED. SOMEONE EVIL.

HE WAS BROUGHT BACK TO LIFE IN THIS WELLHOUSE. AND IF HE RETURNS HERE... IF HE'S EVER DRAGGED, THROWN, OR FORCED THROUGH THIS DOOR...

"...HE'S HISTORY."

DO YOU READ ME, PRIVATE?

SIR, YES SIR.

IT'LL NEVER HAPPEN, SIR. I'M NOT TOUGH ENOUGH. I'M NOT SMART ENOUGH. I'M SORRY, SIR.

THERE'S NOTHING I CAN DO.

THERE IS, THOUGH.

YOU CAN SHARE YOUR INTEL WITH THE LOCKE KIDS. THEY'LL STOP HIM. THEY JUST NEED THE TRUTH.

IF YOU KNOW WHAT'S TRUE AND YOU DON'T ACT ON IT, RUFUS, THAT MAKES YOU HIS ACCOMPLICE.

AND BELIEVE ME, BEING HIS ACCOMPLICE ISN'T ANY SAFER THAN BEING HIS ENEMY.

TAKE IT FROM SOMEONE WHO KNOWS.

RUUUUUUFUS! WHAT ARE YOU DOING OUT HERE?

WE WERE LOOKING ALL OVER FOR YOU!

THE SERGEANT SAID IT WOULD BE ALL RIGHT. WE WERE GATHERING INTELLIGENCE. HE—

—OH. HE'S GONE NOW.

CHEEZ, I HAD TO FIGHT THE WHOLE BATTLE WITHOUT YOU.

I'M SORRY.

AH, IT'S OKAY. WE CAN FIGHT ANOTHER BATTLE ANY TIME.

LISTEN UP, SOLDIER. I HAVE TO TELL YOU SOMETHING THAT COULD CHANGE THE TIDE OF THIS WAR.

ARE YOU FAMILIAR WITH A RECRUIT NAMED ZACK WELLS?

OH, YEAH. I MISS ZACK. HE USED TO COME HERE MORE OFTEN.

THINK AGAIN, PRIVATE.

ZACK WELLS IS A DOUBLE AGENT. HE'S DANGEROUS... THE MOST DANGEROUS ENEMY WE'VE EVER FACED AND WE HAVE TO STOP HIM BEFORE...

WHAT'S UP GUYS? HATE TO INTERRUPT THE WAR, BUT WE HAVE TO GET YOU HOME, ROOF. CURFEW IN TWENTY MINUTES.

HEY, YOU. I THOUGHT COACH WHEDON WAS COMING TO GET RUFUS.

IT SEEMED LIKE A NICE NIGHT FOR A WALK, SO I SAID I'D DO IT. IT JUST STARTED SNOWING.

HAS IT? MAYBE I'LL COME LOOK. WALK YOU AND RUFUS PART OF THE WAY.

OKAY. SURE. I'D LIKE THAT.

I HAVE TO GET MY BOOTS. I'LL BE RIGHT BACK.

MEET YOU OUTSIDE.

AT EASE, DOGFACES!

YOU EVER TALK TO THE LOCKE KIDS OR ANYONE ELSE ABOUT ME, THEY'LL TAKE YOUR MOTHER AWAY AND PUT HER IN JAIL AND YOU'LL NEVER SEE HER AGAIN.

I THOUGHT YOU ALREADY UNDERSTOOD THAT, OR I NEVER WOULD'VE LET YOU COME HERE.

THEY'D HAVE TO PUT YOU IN FOSTER CARE. YOUR DAD ISN'T GOING TO HELP YOU. WHY DO YOU THINK HE JOINED THE AIR FORCE?

TO GET *AWAY* FROM YOU.

THEY'LL PUT YOU IN A STATE HOME, WITH CRIMINALS AND DRUG USERS. YOU KNOW WHAT THOSE KIDS WOULD DO WITH A LITTLE RETARD LIKE YOU?

TEAR YOU APART.

HEY.

HEY.

AND SO... *A HERO FALLS!*

JACK NIFE IS *GONE*... BUT THE WAR *GOES ON!*

EPILOGUE—CAPE COD HOSPITAL, HYANNIS

AUGH. UFF.

SHIT. THINGS ARE BRIGHT.

HEY, BRIAN. WELCOME BACK.

THE DOC TOLD ME MAYBE TODAY OR TOMORROW... YOU'VE BEEN IN AND OUT ALL MONTH. A LITTLE MORE "IN" EVERY DAY.

MM. DUNCAN. WHAT HAPPENED?

THEY SAID YOU MIGHT NOT REMEMBER AT FIRST. THERE WAS A FIGHT. THERE WERE SOME DRUNKS—

NO NO. I REMEMBER THAT. I MEAN, WHAT HAPPENED TO THE SOX? WE HAD A SHOT AT THE PLAYOFFS.

OH... WE FINISHED IN 2ND PLACE. PREDICTABLE. SO YOU REMEMBER WHAT HAPPENED? THEY ARRESTED BOTH OF THEM. THE DRUNKS WHO ATTACKED US IN THE BAR.

GOOD. FUCK 'EM. WHAT ABOUT THE KID WITH THE GUN? THE KID IN THE KITCHEN?

WHAT KID?

100

- KEYS TO THE KINGDOM -

Chapter Five

# DETECTIVES

**Part I**

CAPE COD HOSPITAL, HYANNIS—6 DAYS AGO

SO WHAT WAS IT LIKE? BEING IN A COMA?

I DON'T KNOW.

I DON'T REMEMBER ANYTHING ABOUT IT.

IT'S LIKE I WAS A TV. SOMEONE SWITCHED ME OFF IN SEPTEMBER, TURNED ME BACK ON IN FEBRUARY.

GOOD. I MEAN—NOT GOOD. BUT BETTER THAN BAD DREAMS OR... BEING IN PAIN OR SOMETHING.

I GUESS NOT FEELING ANYTHING—JUST, YOU KNOW, OBLIVION—SOMETIMES IS FOR THE BEST.

ARE YOU OKAY, KIDDO? TRY NOT TO SOUND SO TURNED ON BY THE IDEA OF OBLIVION.

WHAT'S THE HARDEST YOU'VE EVER BEEN LET DOWN?

PROBABLY WHEN THE EAGLES WENT OUT ON THEIR REUNION TOUR. FIVE HUNDRED BUCKS A TICKET AND THEY SUCKED.

HEY, KID. THE GIRL STUFF GETS BETTER AFTER HIGH SCHOOL.

REALLY?

I HAD A LOT OF DIFFICULT RELATIONSHIPS WHEN I WAS YOUR AGE. IT'S HARD TO MAKE RELATIONSHIPS WORK WITH OTHERS WHEN YOU DON'T HAVE A GOOD RELATIONSHIP WITH YOURSELF.

HEY, THAT DIDN'T SOUND TOO DOCTOR PHIL, DID IT?

MAYBE A LITTLE.

WELL. I ASSUME. IT DIDN'T FOR ME, 'CAUSE IT TURNED OUT I WAS GAY, BUT FOR YOU IT SHOULD DEFINITELY IMPROVE.

LOOK, I GOT NINE STAPLES IN MY HEAD NOW. I'M LUCKY I CAN STILL SPELL MY OWN NAME.

IF YOU CAME TO ME LOOKING FOR LITTLE NUGGETS OF WISDOM, CHECK THE BEDPAN.

I WISH YOU'D TAKE IT EASY ON YOURSELF, KIDDO.

THERE'RE TWO NASTY DRUNKS AND THEIR PSYCHO FRIEND WHO TRIED TO GET ME KILLED. IT'S NOT LIKE YOU EVER DID ANYTHING THAT GOT ANYONE KILLED.

HELL-LLO. A COUPLE CAPPUCCINOS FOR TYLER AND ME AND A TALL, DELICIOUSLY COLD GLASS OF PRUNE JUICE FOR YOUNG MR. ROGAN.

PRUNE JUICE. JESUS, DUNCAN, ONLY YOU COULD MAKE ME MISS MY IV DRIP.

SO DID TY TELL YOU HIS BIG NEWS? HE WAS ACCEPTED TO BERKELEY YESTERDAY.

NO SHIT. CONGRATU-FUCKING-LATIONS, TY. THAT'S WHERE YOUR PARENTS MET, ISN'T IT?

YOUR FATHER WOULD BE SO PROUD OF THE MAN YOU'RE BECOMING. OF THE CHOICES YOU'VE MADE.

I CAN'T BELIEVE IT'S GOING TO BE FIVE MORE WEEKS BEFORE I CAN BRING HIM HOME. I CAN'T BELIEVE HE'S BEEN IN THAT LITTLE HOSPITAL ROOM FIVE *MONTHS*.

ON THE BRIGHT SIDE, THOSE BRAINLESS BITCHES WHO RAN HIM DOWN ARE GOING TO BE IN A LITTLE ROOM FOR FIVE *YEARS*, RIGHT?

BALANCE.

THEY COULD HAVE HALF THAT IF THEY'D MAKE A DEAL, TELL US ABOUT THE GUY WHO CAME IN THE HOUSE WITH A GUN. BUT THEY'RE PLAYING STUPID.

I'M SURPRISED THE COPS CAN'T FIND HIM BASED ON BRIAN'S DESCRIPTION.

*ACH.* THERE'RE A THOUSAND DUDES ON CAPE COD WHO LOOK LIKE THE GUY BRIAN SAW. BLACK HAIR. EARLY TWENTIES—MAYBE A TEENAGER EVEN. NOSE RING.

YEAH, BUT STILL. IT'S GOT TO BE SOMEONE THE GIRLS KNEW. A BOYFRIEND OR SOMEONE. A NOSE RING, THAT'S A PRETTY DISTINCTIVE DETAIL.

NOPE. DOESN'T MATCH ANY OF THEIR RELATIVES OR FRIENDS OR—YOU KNOW, I THINK IT WAS A LIP RING, ACTUALLY.

YEAH, THAT'S WHAT BRIAN SAID. RING IN HIS LOWER LIP.

OH, WELL. IT'S OUT OF OUR HANDS. NOT LIKE WE CAN TRACK THE GUY DOWN. WHAT ARE WE, DETECTIVES?

LOVECRAFT—4 DAYS AGO

WHAT? WHAT IS IT?

DO YOU LIKE KISSING ME?

I LIKE WHAT IT MEANS.

WHAT'S IT MEAN?

THAT YOU'RE MINE.

DON'T YOU LIKE BEING KISSED?

IT FEELS GOOD. YOU HAVE NICE BREATH.

WAY TO BUILD ME UP. THAT'S IT? I *TASTE* ALL RIGHT? I FEEL LESS LIKE A BOYFRIEND, MORE LIKE A NEW COUGH SYRUP.

I DON'T KNOW. I NEVER WOULD'VE KISSED YOU IF I DIDN'T TAKE MY FEAR OUT OF MY HEAD. *BUT*, I THINK WITHOUT THE FEAR PART, MAYBE KISSING ISN'T AS... EXCITING AS IT SHOULD BE.

IT'S LIKE SAYING I LOVE YOU. I WASN'T AFRAID TO SAY IT. BUT... MAYBE THAT MAKES IT MEAN LESS.

MEANS EVERYTHING TO ME.

GO SHOW HOW FEARLESS YOU ARE AND ASK YOUR BRO TO LET US HELP HIM. I'M NOT GOING TO DO IT.

WAVE. HE'S WATCHING US.

SCARY.

I WOULDN'T KNOW.

SHIT. RIGHT IN FRONT OF MY FACE.

STILL. YOU SHOULD... NOT BE ALONE. ON A BIG NIGHT. YOU HAVE THESE WALLS UP. TO PROTECT YOURSELF. TO PROTECT EVERYONE ELSE.

YOU DON'T HAVE TO DEAL WITH EVERYTHING ALONE. YOU DON'T HAVE TO BE ALONE.

WHERE YOU GOING WITH THIS, KINSEY?

YOU'RE THE ONLY ONE THAT KNOWS WHERE THE OMEGA KEY IS. THE DARK LADY SEEMS TO KNOW IT, TOO. THAT'S WHY ALL HER ATTACKS CENTER ON YOU. LET ME HELP.

I COULD HAVE A TURN HIDING IT. ZACK COULD HAVE A TURN—

HE CARES ABOUT YOU. THAT'S WHAT HE HAS TO DO WITH IT.

WHAT'S ZACK GOT TO DO WITH IT?

DID HE ASK ABOUT HELPING OUT WITH THE OMEGA KEY?

NO. YES. I DON'T KNOW. I THINK I SUGGESTED IT. THAT'S NOT THE POINT. THE POINT IS, HE'S READY TO HELP. HE WANTS TO HELP.

I DON'T KNOW HOW MUCH HE COULD DO. HE'S ALWAYS AWAY, WORKING ON HIS BIG RESEARCH PAPER IN BOSTON.

JUST ON WEEKENDS.

YEAH. I'VE NOTICED.

DUDE, WHERE **ARE** YOU THESE DAYS? WE NEVER HANG OUT ANYMORE. SOMETHING I DID?

SEARCH YOUR CONSCIENCE.

DON'T HAVE ONE.

HA.

HEY. NO SHITTING AROUND— ARE YOU OKAY? YOU'VE BEEN KEEPING TO YOURSELF A LOT AND—

JUST GOT THIS LECTURE FROM KINSEY THE OTHER DAY, SO YOU CAN SPARE ME. I'M NOT GOING TO OFF MYSELF. JUST NOT FEELING SOCIAL.

SEEMS LIKE YOU'VE BEEN DEPRESSED EVER SINCE YOU GOT BACK FROM CAPE COD. HOW WAS IT, ANYWAY? SEEING DUNCAN AND HIS FRIEND AND ALL?

BRIAN. WELL, HE'S GOT NINE STAPLES IN HIS HEAD, AND AN EXTERNAL CAST ON HIS RIGHT LEG AND HE CAN'T REMEMBER SOME THINGS.

LIKE THE STREET HE GREW UP ON OR THE NAME OF HIS CAT. BUT HE'S OKAY.

WHAT ABOUT THE LADIES WHO ATTACKED HIM? HE REMEMBER MUCH ABOUT THAT?

NO.

I SPENT ALL WINTER ON ICE SKATES AND IT SUCKED. TELL ME WHY WE'RE HERE AGAIN?

TO LOOK AT GIRLS IN THEIR LITTLE SKIRTS. CHECK OUT STRAWBERRY THERE. THE REDHEAD.

YOU'RE DATING MY SISTER. SHOW SOME CLASS.

I'LL TRY. I JUST GOT A LOT OF DOG IN ME.

HALF WOLF?

DEFINITELY. HEY, BODE, LET ME—

I LOVE THIS. IT'S LIKE FLYING. IT'S LIKE BEING DEAD AGAIN. LIKE BEING A GHOST. I WAS A GHOST ONCE, YOU KNOW? I MISS BEING DEAD. IT WAS REALLY FUN.

AW, KID. YOU'RE A SCREAM.

ALLEZ.

LOVECRAFT—TODAY

KLIK

LOVECRAFT    GROTON
00          00

WELLS
LOVECRAFT

CAN I HAVE NACHOS?

I TOLD YOU, NO CRAP BEFORE DINNER. WE'VE GOT LASAGNA AT HOME.

CHIK!

LOVECRAFT 03    GROTON 00

LOOK, HE DOESN'T EVEN NEED TO PARRY! DODGE, DODGE, DODGE... ALL ZACK DOES IS DODGE.

HE'S A SLIPPERY WANKER, ALL RIGHT. I'LL GIVE HIM THAT.

UNH!

LOVECRAFT 04    GROTON 00

I'LL WALK HOME WITH BODE, FIX HIM UP WITH DINNER. IT'S IN THE WARMER, RIGHT?

TYLER, THE TOURNEY JUST STARTED. ZACK HAS TWO MORE MATCHES.

LET ME KNOW HOW ZORRO MAKES OUT, OKAY?

LOVECRAFT  GROTON
05  00

HEY, TY! TY! I WAS WONDERING SOMETHING!

YEAH?

DO YOU THINK YOU CAN TEACH A MONKEY TO KUNG FU? THEY TAUGHT ONE SIGN LANGUAGE, I SAW IT ON DISCOVERY.

ALSO, MY FRIEND JAY SAYS THEY SENT A CHIMPANZEE INTO OUTER SPACE, AND I WAS WONDERING—IS HE STILL THERE? WHAT'S HE DOING UP THERE?

WHERE ARE WE?

THIS IS WHERE ZACK AND RUFUS LIVE. YOU SHOULD GIVE RUFUS HIS BUSTED ACTION FIGURE BACK.

93

COME ON IN! DOOR'S OPEN!

TYLER!

HI, MRS. WHEDON.

WE WERE IN THE NEIGHBORHOOD AND RUFUS LEFT HIS ACTION FIGURE AT OUR HOUSE. IT'S KIND OF BUSTED UP, BUT WE FIGURED HE MIGHT WANT IT BACK.

HE'LL BE GLAD TO SEE GOOD OL' JACK NIFE. THAT'S ONE OF HIS FAVORITES.

I JUST MADE COOKIES. THEY'RE STILL HOT.

CAN I HAVE ONE?

DON'T TELL MOM I LET YOU.

MA'AM? I ALSO FORGOT TO COPY DOWN THE ETHICS READING. CAN I RUN UP TO ZACK'S ROOM AND CHECK HIS NOTEBOOK?

OH, I DON'T SEE WHY NOT.

BODE, DO YOU WANT TO BRING RUFUS HIS ACTION FIGURE AND A COOKIE?

YES, MA'AM.

HEY, UH... MISS WHEDON? I JUST WANTED TO SAY, IT'S PRETTY COOL YOU AGREED TO LET YOUR NEPHEW STAY WITH YOU ALL YEAR.

I GUESS YOU AND ZACK HAVE A REAL SPECIAL RELATIONSHIP.

BE HONEST— HOW GREAT WAS I?

DON'T GET COCKY. YOU'VE GOT TWO MORE MATCHES.

WHERE'D TYLER AND BODE GO?

I KNOW IT'S HARD TO BELIEVE, BUT NOT EVERYONE CAN PUT THEIR LIFE ON HOLD TO WATCH YOU STAB PEOPLE. HE'S TAKING BODE HOME. HE'S BEEN MOODY. HE'S OBSESSED WITH THE DARK LADY. YOU KNOW WHAT HE'S BEEN DOING?

HE MADE A CALENDAR OF EVERY TIME WE HAD TO FIGHT THE DARK LADY IN FEBRUARY. I'M, LIKE, *WHY?*

BUT HE DOESN'T SAY BECAUSE HE'S COMPLETELY PARANOID. HE DOESN'T TRUST ANYONE SINCE JORDAN BROKE UP WITH HIM, NOT ME, NOT YOU, NOT—

—WHAT'S UP? WHERE YOU GOING? YOU HAVE ANOTHER MATCH IN A COUPLE.

I KNOW. I BETTER HURRY IF I'M GOING TO HIT THE CAN.

LOCKER ROO

I DON'T GET IT. I DON'T UNDERSTAND WHAT GOT YOU LOOKING MY WAY.

I WAS SO CAREFUL AND— NO OFFENSE, TY— YOU AREN'T EXACTLY SHERLOCK HOLMES.

BALLS.

THAT'S THE BEST YOU GOT? BALLS?

SEE, THIS IS WHAT I MEAN. YOUR DAD WAS A THINKER. BUT YOU'RE JUST A DUMBASS JOCK. EVEN YOUR INSULTS ARE DUMBASS.

CLIC

I'M NOT INSULTING YOU. I'M ANSWERING YOUR QUESTION ABOUT WHAT GOT ME LOOKING YOUR WAY.

YOU ATTACKED US IN THE WOODS AS A DOG AND WHEN I WAS WRESTLING YOU OFF ME, I NOTICED NUTS.

IT GOT ME THINKING THAT IF THERE'S A KEY TO CHANGE YOU INTO AN ANIMAL, OR TO CHANGE YOUR SIZE, THERE MIGHT BE ONE TO CHANGE YOUR GENDER.

SO I STARTED THINKING, WHAT IF THE DARK LADY IS ACTUALLY A DARK GUY?

DON'T MOVE.

...DON'T MOVE, DON'T MOVE, DON'T MOVE ALONG... STAY WHERE YOU ARE, THIS IS THE "DON'T MOVE" SONG...

CHONG
CHANG
CHONG

DON'T MAKE ME POP YOUR EYEBALL OUT.

SOUNDS LIKE SOMEONE'S HERE. YOU GOING TO CUT ME UP WHILE YOU'VE GOT VISITORS?

DON'T MOVE.

♪ ...DON'T MOVE, DON'T MOVE, STAY LIKE YOU'RE STUCK WITH A TACK... DON'T MOVE, DON'T MOVE, DODGE WILL KILL YOU WHEN HE GETS BACK... ♪

AUNTIE ELLIE! WHO'S THAT?

ZACK? WHEN DID YOU GET HERE? DID YOU SNEAK IN THROUGH THE BACK DOOR WHEN I WASN'T LOOKING?

THAT BOY. COMES AND GOES AT ALL HOURS, AS HE PLEASES, NEVER SEE HIM WALKING IN, NEVER SEE HIM WALKING OUT.

I SWEAR, SOMETIMES IT'S ALMOST LIKE MAGIC.

LOVECRAFT—FIVE DAYS AGO

THERE SHE IS AGAIN.

HM? THERE WHO IS?

ELLIE WHEDON. TRACK COACH OVER AT THE ACADEMY.

SHE COMES OUT AND LIGHTS THE MEMORY CANDLES FOR HIM EVERY NIGHT.

FOOLISH TO THINK ANYONE WOULD BELIEVE IT WAS SUICIDE. IF HE WAS GOING TO KILL HIMSELF, HE WOULD'VE USED THOSE PILLS AND THE ABUNDANT ALCOHOL AT HAND.

SO MUCH MORE PEACEFUL THAN THE GUN.

THEY OUGHT TO HAVE FUNERALS FOR TEACHERS LIKE THEY HAVE FUNERALS FOR COPS, DON'T YOU THINK? PUT ON A SHOW.

YOU KNOW HOW COPS GET A RIFLE SALUTE? TEACHERS OUGHT TO HAVE SOMETHING.

THEY COULD PASS OUT A MULTIPLE CHOICE TEST AT THE MEMORIAL SERVICE. YOU HAVE TO FILL IT OUT WITH A NUMBER TWO PENCIL, SHOW WHAT YOU REMEMBER ABOUT THE DECEASED.

INSTEAD, ALL THIS GUY GETS IS EIGHT LOUSY CANDLES AND ONE DEPRESSED TRACK COACH. TEACHERS HAVE A SHIT DEAL.

126

YOU SEE ANYTHING YOU DIDN'T SEE ALL THE OTHER TIMES WE'VE BEEN IN HERE?

NO. AND TOMORROW, JOSEPH RIDGEWAY'S OLDEST SON WILL COME AND PACK EVERYTHING AWAY AND IT WON'T BE A CRIME SCENE ANYMORE.

IT WILL BE FACULTY HOUSING. AND JOE RIDGEWAY'S MURDER WILL BE SHUFFLED AWAY INTO THE COLD CASE FILE.

SIR? IF THERE WAS ANYTHING TO FIND IN THIS ROOM, YOU WOULD'VE FOUND IT.

YOU GOT BLOOD. YOU GOT DNA. YOU KNOW RIDGEWAY DIDN'T KILL HIMSELF.

THIS ROOM GAVE YOU EVERYTHING IT HAD. WHAT YOU'RE LOOKING FOR IS OUT THERE. I DON'T KNOW WHERE. BUT **SOMEWHERE**.

YES. I'M SURE YOU'RE RIGHT. WHAT I'M LOOKING FOR IS PROBABLY OUT THERE...

...YOU SAY SHE COMES EVERY NIGHT? WHY DO YOU THINK THAT IS? WERE THEY CLOSE?

PRETTY CLOSE, I GUESS. SHE WAS HIS STUDENT BEFORE THEY WERE TEACHERS TOGETHER. ALSO SHE MIGHT BE FEELING ESPECIALLY SENSITIVE RIGHT NOW.

HER MOTHER WAS JOE RIDGEWAY'S AGE, AND SHE JUST DIED, TOO. LAST SPRING, IN THAT ACCIDENT UP AT SOGGY COVE. RIGHT BEHIND KEYHOUSE.

WHAT ACCIDENT?

YES, IS THIS THE WHEDON RESIDENCE? MY NAME IS DETECTIVE MUTUKU, WITH THE MASSACHUSETTS STATE POLICE.

COULD I SPEAK TO YOUR MOTHER, SON?

MY MOTHER ISN'T HERE. SHE'S AT WORK. I'M AT HOME WITH ZACK.

ARE YOU GOING TO ARREST HER? ZACK SAYS IF YOU ARREST HER, I'LL HAVE TO GO TO FOSTER CARE.

YOUR MOTHER ISN'T IN TROUBLE, SON. I JUST WANTED TO TALK TO HER. WHO IS THIS ZACK PERSON? WHY WOULD HE SAY SOMETHING LIKE THAT TO YOU?

ROOF! WHO'S ON THE PHONE?

SOMEONE FOR MOM!

TELL 'EM TO CALL BACK!

ZACK SAYS I HAVE TO GO. IF HE KNEW I WAS TALKING TO A POLICEMAN HE'D BE REALLY MAD. GOODBYE.

LOVECRAFT, MASSACHUSETTS—NOW

ZACK? MR. MUTUKU WANTS TO TALK TO ME ABOUT—WELL, I DON'T KNOW WHAT ABOUT. DO YOU WANT TO GIVE US A MOMENT TO...

IT WON'T BE NECESSARY TO SPEAK PRIVATELY, MS. WHEDON. I'D LIKE TO TALK TO ZACK AS MUCH AS I'D LIKE TO TALK TO YOU.

ALL RIGHT. I HOPE NO ONE'S IN TROUBLE.

OH, NOT AT ALL. I'VE JUST BEEN INTERVIEWING PEOPLE WHO KNEW JOE RIDGEWAY. DID YOU KNOW HIM, ZACK?

YOU MEAN THE TEACHER WHO DIED, LIKE, LAST YEAR?

NO. MY GIRLFRIEND HAD A CLASS WITH HIM AND THOUGHT HE WAS A REAL SWEET OLD DUDE. SHE LIKED HIS BOW TIES. I'M SORRY I NEVER HAD A CHANCE TO GET TO KNOW HIM.

WHAT ABOUT CANDICE WHEDON? ELLIE'S MOTHER? DID YOU KNOW HER WELL, ZACK? WAS SHE A REAL SWEET OLD LADY?

YOU SHOULDN'T DO THAT, YOU KNOW?

DO WHAT?

SHAKE HANDS WITH A GUY YOU THINK MAYBE MURDERED A FEW PEOPLE. NOT WHEN HE'S HOLDING A KNIFE.

THERE'S NOWHERE TO GO, ZACK. UNLESS YOU KNOW HOW TO FLY, THERE'S NO WAY OUT FOR YOU UP THERE.

THANKS FOR THE TIP.

SON. YOU NEED TO LEAVE THIS HOUSE.

LET GO OF ME.

MOM? MOM?

WHAT THE HELL IS GOING ON?

HOW DO YOU LIKE THAT, LUV? ZACK HAS VANISHED, PERHAPS, ONE HOPES, NEVER TO RETURN.

ALTHOUGH IF HE DOESN'T SHOW UP IN ANOTHER FIVE MINUTES, WE'LL HAVE TO FORFEIT. THERE GOES THE UNDEFEATED SEASON. PISSER.

WHAT ARE YOU DOING?

THIS ISN'T RIGHT.

I'M GOING OUTSIDE. THERE'S A BETTER SIGNAL OUT THERE. I'M GOING TO FIND OUT WHERE HE WENT AND WHAT HE'S DOING.

HE BETTER BE ABLE TO EXPLAIN HIMSELF OR HE'S A DEAD MAN.

WHY AREN'T YOU ANSWERING YOUR DAMN CELL PHONE?

MAYBE YOU WENT HOME?

I HAVE TO ANSWER THE PHONE. I'LL COME BACK.

CHEEP CHEEP CHEEP

HELLO? OH, HI, KINSEY. ZACK?

HE JUST KILLED MY MOTHER. NOW HE'S FLYING AWAY WITH BODE.

WAIT, IT LOOKS LIKE THEY'RE LANDING.

ZACK AND BODE ARE GOING AWAY NOW. ZACK IS MAKING BODE DISAPPEAR.

ALL RIGHT, KINSEY. I'LL TALK TO YOU LATER. I'M GOING TO SIT WITH MY MOTHER. SHE SHOULDN'T BE ALONE.

144

...to be continued in Locke & Key: CLOCKWORKS

Edited by **Chris Ryall**
Lettered by **Robbie Robbins**
Colored by **Jay Fotos**
Storytellers **Joe Hill** & **Gabriel Rodríguez**

Locke & Key created by JOE HILL & GABRIEL RODRÍGUEZ

*in our ...*
*& I resolv ...*
*hazzarded such a f...*
*long I work'd in a for...*
*till finallie t'was cast...*
*oh how, I feer'd! M...*
*in the gather...*
*straked o...*
*held the d...*
*beig'd G...*
*Gou...*
*ho...*

# THE KNOWN KEYS
(EXCERPTS FROM THE DIARY OF
BENJAMIN PIERCE LOCKE, 1757 - 1799)

## GHoST KeY

onlee in occaisonull daith do I find peece now, for with the bode caste aisyde, it is possibull for one to know his own ETERNALL SOULE. My spairt cannot leeve the grounds of Keyhowse, but heyre I walke laik an aingel! I aim everywhare and nowhare at once, from the tall's towair, to the deepst caves. It is hard to dreem thair could be any dore more terryble or wondairfulle than that wych dyvydes deth from lyfe, yet my expairances at the thraishold of the black dore have teach'd me thair are worse things than to dyye...

## eCHo KeY

whence I unlock'd the dore I heerd a voice that saimed to ecko from the well & it aisk'd me who I sat & I spake of my brother. No sooner had the words pass'd my lips thence he ROSE from the WELL like a spairt & yet was living flaish, alltho he had dyed in the Drowning Caves not 6 weeks beefor. He clasp'd me to his bosom & sayd why do ye look so unhappy to see me brother, but I wast in feer for my allmaighty SOUL & fled to the howse & pray'd thair to the LORD
But in that grait howse, an ecko of my voice was all the reeply I receiv'd

## aNYWHeRe KeY

us'd the key to anyplaice againe, to return to Boston, & gaither intelaigents for Crais. Tis an act of terryble wychcraift, but better I do it, than my sister, who is obssaissed with REVENGING herself upon the RED-COATS, for thair violence agin our faither & brother & belov'd maither. Aye, my dredd of beeing called to acconut someday by SATAN HIMSELF is a trifling concern when maiched with my desyre to rid the worlde of the devylls who taik the King's Coyne to do raip & murdur...

## HeaD KeY

of alle the keys I have forged from the WHISP'RING IRON, 'tis the key that opens the human mind I most regrait. Miranda hast a pervairse fasinaytion whist the key & hast us'd ait to fill her head with all thair is to know about WAR & the SLAIYING of MEN, & she carrys an arsanall whist her whairever she goes. Yet I am less in dred of what she has put in than what she hast remov'd. Sometimes it is as if she is now without FEER and indeed is herself more man than I!

## GeNDeR KeY

my sister - or should I now say my brother! - fights the shadow war with Crais in the streets of Boston whilst I wait at home, like a helpless maiden, praying to the ALLMAIGHTY! for her safe return. When first I fashin'd the key, I imaguined she maight trainsform to a boy to protect her, if necessaire, from the unsavorie lusts of ENGLISHMEN should the King's foot-soldiers return to Lovecraft to abuse God fairing womain. Never did I think she wouldst WILLENGLY caist off the wardrobe of her femininitie for this ruggaid liberation among men...

## SHaDoW KeY

O Wycked Night! Damn'd be Crais & Damn'd be the Redcoats & Damn'd be my own foole self. Miranda tis griev'sly hurt & lingers on the thraishold of deth! The Redcoats pursued her & the tattr'd reminante of Crais's companie into the caves but I drove them back with the aide of the lyving shadows. If she dies I wouldst rather be a shadow myself than remain in thys diabollicall world, knowing she wouldst never have been at riske if not for me!

## GiaNT KeY

she is dying & thair is nothing I can do to save her!
The Redcoats return'd to assalle the house & claym her & I admitte I lette my fury & miserie get the better of me. I used the giant's key to multiplie my syze, so that my body was as vaste as my hayte & I turn'd upon a wholle regiment & ~ O GOD forgive me! ~ did detestably murther them alle!

## MENDiNG KEY

the Iron whisper'd to me laste night & I worked in a fever alle day, mayking a cabinet & forging a new key out of that dreadfull metal that is not metal. Yet if the devil may pervairt Holie Scripture to serve his purposes, so may the rihteous at times turn the DEVILLS TOOLS to do the work of SWEET JESU! For the key & cabinet I fashin'd could be used to mend fraicturd objykts ~ shatter'd plattes, crack'd eggs & broken sistairs. Bless'd be THE LORD, Miranda hast recovr'd! I only wish she wouldst remembair her place & become the demure & modestte girlle she once was, but fear her love for Crais will emperille her againe soon enough...

## Animal Key

**September 9th, 1851~**

...Ulysses said he would fly all the way to Hell if he had to, to find Delacorte for me. Clint said he would probably only be required to fly to Georgia, but that the two places were much alike, except Georgia is a bit hotter. We have fought a thousand times, my brothers and I, but this morning I felt I could not love any living souls more. Ulysses stepped through the door, and emerged on the other side, a golden eagle. He gave me a short, lordly look, and took to the skies...

## Music Box Key

**November 3rd, 1851~**

...he was dying fast from his injuries and knew it. He said he would go to glory and take his secrets with him. Ulysses said that if our Lord meant to open the Gates Of Heaven to a B---- like him, he would prefer to throw in with the Devil. Clint hissed and seemed ready to strike again, but I restrained him. I knew if Hammersmith died, I would likely never see Delacorte again, and so I turned the Key in the Music Box, and the tune began to play. A miniature version of myself turned around and around, and sang:

...tell us who paid you for the girl...

...do it now before you leave this world...

Hammersmith's eyes widened, and he began to speak...

## Skin Key

**November 5th, 1851~**

...I looked into the mirror, and turned it, so I became of the African race, and my skin was dark as coal. And it is a wonderment to me. All my thoughts had, until then, been bent on finding Delacorte and beseeching her to become free and white like myself. But when I saw my black features in the mirror, I was surprised to find I liked my own face better than I had ever liked it before. Ulysses considered me for the longest of times, before offering me my hat and saying "Remember to keep your eyes down, Harland. You have the White Man's habit of meeting another man's gaze, but you will fare poorly if you behave that way here in Georgia."

## Engels-Schlüssel

### 4. Juni 1942

Mein Gott. Mein Gott! Bei Tagesanbruch war ich draußen und suchte nach dem kleinen Joe. Es stürmte und regnete in Strömen. Alles kam mir krank und unwirklich vor – wie in einem Albtraum. Ich rannte und rannte, völlig verzweifelt, und es war mir scheißegal, was er Jean über mich erzählte. Wenn er tot war, wollte ich selbst auch sterben. Und dann sah ich etwas Unglaubliches - etwas, das es gar nicht hätte geben dürfen, und ich bekam vor Überraschung und Staunen ganz weiche Knie. Ich sah Jean durch den Regen hinauffliegen, den zerschlagenen Körper ihres Bruders in den Armen. Sie trug das Gurtzeug mit den Flügeln, und hintendrin steckte der Schlüssel. Ich schwöre, sie ist geflogen! Und dabei sah sie so wunderschön aus wie eine Trauertaube.

## Philosophoscope Key

### July 3rd, 1942

...Hannes asked me to come with him, in his quiet inflected English. I told him I liked it better when I thought he was mute because at least then he couldn't tell me lies. But I took his hand and went with him. He walked me to the Philosophoscope in the tower. Once I realized where we were going, Johnnie. I didn't want to go, and couldn't help myself. Once I realized what he was going to show me. He put the Key in, and shifted the lever to TruestLove and asked me to look. Oh Johnnie. How I have lied to myself for months. He knew what I would see somehow even when I didn't... that I would see him...

## Herkules-Schlüssel

### 13. Juli 1942

Die Hälfte der 8. Armee und ein schier endloser Haufen SS-Männer warteten da auf mich! Ich schleuderte Eric gegen die Mauer und hörte, wie seine Rippen brachen, als wäre jemand auf ein Bündel Zweige gesprungen. Ich muss zugeben, das hörte sich wie Musik in meinen Ohren an! Mit der anderen Hand schlug ich nach den Soldaten, und sie flogen wie Streichhölzer durch die Luft. Der Herkules-Schlüssel setzte all die Kraft in mir frei, die ich als verdammter Krüppel nie gehabt hatte. Aber der Sturmbannführer wusste, wie er mich fertigmachen konnte!